YAKALOU MEDIA

The Smart Couple's Guide to Moving In Together

The 150 Most Important Questions Every Smart Couples Must Ask Before Moving in Together

Copyright © 2023 by Yakalou Media

All rights reserved. No part of this publication may be reproduced, stored or transmitted in any form or by any means, electronic, mechanical, photocopying, recording, scanning, or otherwise without written permission from the publisher. It is illegal to copy this book, post it to a website, or distribute it by any other means without permission.

First edition

This book was professionally typeset on Reedsy. Find out more at reedsy.com

Contents

Disclaimer   v

I   Part - 1: Setting the Stage

Introduction   3
How Important Is This Book And What You Will Learn From It?   5
How To Use This Book To Get The Most Out Of It?   7
How Do You Start The Conversation?   9
What Are The Do's And Don'ts? And A Word Of Warning!   11

II   Part - 2: 100 Insightful Must-Ask Questions Before Moving In With Your Partner

Chapter 1: Financial Matters   17
Chapter 2: Household Responsibilities   20
Chapter 3: Personal Habits   23
Chapter 4: Future Goals   26
Chapter 5: Family and Friends   28
Chapter 6: Conflict Resolution   31
Chapter 7: Space and Privacy   34
Chapter 8: Communication   37
Chapter 9: Shared Activities   40

Chapter 10: Intimacy and Affection	43
Chapter 11: Health and Medical conditions	45
Chapter 12: Career Conversations	48
Chapter 13: Overnight Guests	50
Chapter 14: Pets	53
Chapter 15: Breaking Up and Moving Out	55
Conclusion: The Journey Continues...	58

III   Part – 3: Bonus Chapters

The Moving Checklist: From 8 Weeks Before to 4 Weeks After	63
The 50 Must-Have Essentials & Tools Before Moving In	69
The 100 Must-Have Items You Need After Moving In	74
120 Money Questions To Understand Each Other Financial...	81
The 30 Questions To Ask Yourself Before Everything &...	88

Disclaimer

This book is designed to provide information only. This information is provided and sold with the knowledge that the publisher and author do not offer any legal or other professional advice. In the case of a need for any such expertise, consult with the appropriate professional.

This book does not contain all the information available on the subject. This book has not been created to be specific to any individual's or organization's situation or needs. Every effort has been made to make this book as accurate as possible. However, there may be typographical and/or content errors. Therefore, this book should serve only as a general guide, not as the ultimate source of subject information.

This book contains information that might be dated and is intended only to educate and entertain. Regarding any loss or damage allegedly suffered or alleged to have occurred as a result of the information in this book, either directly or indirectly, the author and publisher shall have no liability or responsibility to any person or entity.

I

Part - 1: Setting the Stage

Part 1 of this book serves as a foundational guide to navigating the contents and purpose of this book. It emphasizes the significance of the material, offers strategies for optimal utilization, and provides essential advice on initiating conversations about cohabitation, ensuring you approach the topic with care, understanding, and foresight.

Introduction

Have you ever found yourself staring at a box of your partner's forgotten belongings and wondered, "Did we even discuss this?" Moving in together is like opening a Pandora's box of revelations. Some are delightful surprises—like discovering you both love waking up to the smell of freshly brewed coffee. But others? Not so much. Like finding out that one of you is a morning person and the other could moonlight as a night owl. Or that "clean" has entirely different definitions in your respective dictionaries.

Wouldn't it be easier if we could lay it all out on the table before the move? Before the first sock is left on the floor or the first toothpaste cap is mysteriously left off? What if there was a guide, a set of compass points, to steer your journey together?

In "The Smart Couple's Guide to Moving In Together", that's precisely what we aim to offer. Why leave the future to a game of chance when you can navigate it together, fully prepared? After all, isn't a strong relationship built on understanding, clarity, and open communication? Dive into these questions, sit down with your partner, and embark on an enlightening journey of discovery. Because, before sharing a home, it's essential to share your truths, dreams, quirks, and—yes—even your preferred brand of toothpaste.

Ready to transition from guessing to knowing? Let's get

started!

How Important Is This Book And What You Will Learn From It?

Have you ever played a game without knowing the rules? If you have, you'll know it's a mix of confusion, hilarity, and sometimes, frustration. That's a bit like moving in with someone without discussing the essentials first. It might seem fun initially as you navigate through the uncharted waters, but soon the tides of misunderstandings can rise, leading to choppy waters. This book is your rulebook, the guide to ensure that the game of cohabitation is more joy than jeopardy.

So, why is this book essential?

First, understanding is the cornerstone of a harmonious life together. By asking these questions, you're not just seeking answers but also understanding your partner's perspective. The "whys" behind their answers are as crucial as the answers themselves. Why do they like their towels folded a certain way? Perhaps it's a cherished memory from childhood or just a personal quirk. The key is in the details. And details matter.

Next, preemptive conversations can prevent potential conflicts. You're setting expectations by addressing critical topics like finances or family visits. No more surprise arguments about unwashed dishes or unscheduled visits from in-laws. Instead, you get a roadmap that showcases both of your preferences, allowing for compromises and mutual decisions.

But more than anything, these questions lead to deeper connections. As you journey through this book, you won't just learn about your partner's favorite cereal or views on joint bank accounts. You'll dive deeper into their dreams, fears, and aspirations. These aren't just questions; they're bridges to intimacy.

What will you gain from this book?

1. Clarity: A clear understanding reduces ambiguities. You'll find out where you both align and where you differ, which is just as crucial.

2. Insight: Delving into topics like future plans and personal habits provides a window into your partner's soul.

3. Communication Skills: The art of asking the right questions is a skill. This process will not only equip you with answers but also with the ability to communicate more effectively.

4. Preparedness: Forewarned is forearmed. Knowing the potential challenges ahead allows you to devise strategies to face them together.

5. Strengthened Bond: Every question you ask and answer knits you two closer, weaving a tighter bond of trust and understanding.

Essentially, "The Smart Couple's Guide to Moving In Together" is more than a list of questions. It's a passport to a harmonious shared life, a catalyst for connection, and a tool for crafting the perfect home together. Ready to dive deeper? Let the journey of discovery commence!

How To Use This Book To Get The Most Out Of It?

Remember the last time you got a new gadget or toy? Did you dive in headfirst, playing around until you figured things out, or did you methodically skim the instruction manual first? This book, while less mechanical, offers a guide to understanding the intricate facets of your partner's world. So, how can you use it effectively to ensure you're not just skimming the surface but diving deep into its potential?

Have you ever thought about why we often avoid asking certain questions? Is it fear of the answers, apprehension about prying, or simply not knowing where to start? The first step to utilizing this book is to rid yourself of these inhibitions. Recognize that every question here is a bridge to understanding, not an intrusion.

Pacing is essential!

You don't marathon your favorite TV series in one sitting just because it's all available (or maybe you do, and that's okay too). Treat these questions similarly. Schedule regular sit-downs with your partner where you tackle a few at a time. These moments can be as casual as a coffee chat or as formal as a date night. Setting a conducive environment ensures you both feel relaxed and open to discussing.

Moreover, remember that context is crucial. Asking about financial matters after a stressful day at work might not yield the most open conversation. Timing, as they say, is everything. How can you make sure the setting and mood are right for each topic?

While working through the questions, be an active listener. It's not about waiting for your turn to answer or defend a point. It's about understanding. Delve deeper when a response intrigues or confuses you. A simple, "Can you tell me more about that?" can illuminate hidden layers.

But what if you stumble upon disagreements or touchy subjects? It's natural, and that's okay. This book's purpose isn't to ensure you agree on everything but to provide clarity on where you both stand. Finding disagreements is not a failure; it's an opportunity. After all, isn't growth about identifying areas of improvement and working on them?

Lastly, revisit these questions. People change, circumstances shift, and answers evolve. Make it a tradition, perhaps an annual one, to go back and see how your responses might have morphed over time. It's not just about the initial clarity but also fostering continued understanding.

In essence, this book isn't just a set of questions. It's an evolving dialogue between two people who are committing to a shared journey. By pacing yourself, choosing the right moments, actively listening, and embracing differences, you're ensuring that this journey is not only enlightening but also deeply enriching. Ready to turn the page and start the conversation? Your relationship playbook awaits.

How Do You Start The Conversation?

Have you ever found yourself at the edge of a diving board, gazing down at the water, gathering the courage to leap? Starting challenging conversations can feel a bit like that moment—filled with anticipation, a touch of anxiety, and the promise of a rewarding experience. But how do you muster the courage to jump into such discussions with your partner? How can you broach subjects that might seem awkward or sensitive?

Let's start by asking, Why is initiating the conversation so daunting? Is it because we fear our partner's reaction, or perhaps it's the uncertainty of where the conversation might lead? Whatever the reason, understanding that hesitation is the first step to overcoming it. And the next step? It's setting the stage.

Think about your favorite restaurant or café. What makes it special? Is it the ambient lighting, the soft background music, or maybe the comfortable chairs? Creating a similar comfortable environment for your discussions can make a world of difference. So, where's that special spot for both of you? Perhaps it's your cozy living room or that bench in the nearby park where you've shared countless chats. Finding a setting where you both feel at ease will naturally pave the way for open dialogue.

But is ambiance enough? What about timing?

Have you ever tried discussing something important when either of you is hungry, tired, or distracted? It rarely goes well. Thus, picking a time when you're both relaxed and present is crucial. Maybe after a leisurely Sunday brunch or during a quiet evening walk? When do both of you feel most connected and receptive?

Starting with lighter, non-confrontational topics can also be a wise strategy. You wouldn't start a meal with the heaviest dish, would you? Ease into the more challenging questions. Start with fun topics, like hobbies or travel, before diving into the weightier subjects. This gradual approach can help warm up the conversation, making it easier to delve into deeper issues.

Another essential ingredient? Vulnerability.

It's like opening a window to your soul, letting in fresh air and light. Being honest about your apprehensions can actually make the process smoother. A simple, "I'm a bit nervous about discussing this, but it's important to me," can set a tone of empathy and understanding.

Remember, it's not a one-time event. It's a journey. Some talks will flow effortlessly, while others might require multiple attempts. And that's okay. The goal isn't to rush through the questions but to genuinely understand and be understood.

Starting the conversation is a blend of the right environment, timing, approach, and openness. It's about creating a space where two hearts can share, learn, and grow. So, are you ready to take that leap? With this guide in hand and your partner by your side, you're poised for a rewarding dive into understanding and intimacy. Let the conversation begin!

What Are The Do's And Don'ts? And A Word Of Warning!

You know when you buy a shiny new appliance, and it comes with a manual? Buried within its pages, between how-to-use and maintenance tips, there's often a section on safety guidelines. While this book isn't about operating machinery, the journey you're embarking on is equally crucial, if not more so. Navigating the dynamics of a shared life can sometimes require its own set of safety guidelines. So, what are the do's and don'ts when discussing these pivotal questions? And what should you be cautious about?

The Do's:

- **1. Listen Actively:** You know when someone's speaking, but you're just waiting for your turn? That's not listening. Genuine listening means absorbing, processing, and reflecting on what's being said. Have you ever noticed how different conversations become when we truly hear them?
- **2. Be Patient:** Rome wasn't built in a day, and neither is mutual understanding. Some topics will require more time and revisiting. Can you give your partner that time?
- **3. Embrace Emotion:** Emotions add color to our lives, even

the challenging ones. Allow yourselves to feel, express, and validate each other's feelings. Isn't the journey about understanding the heart as well as the mind?
- **4. Seek Clarification:** If something isn't clear, ask. Simple, right? But how often do we make assumptions instead?

The Don'ts:

- **1. Don't Interrupt:** Remember the frustration when someone cuts you off mid-sentence? Let your partner finish their thought. It's a sign of respect and gives clarity.
- **2. Don't Make It a Debate:** This isn't about winning an argument. It's about understanding. Instead of proving a point, how about finding a meeting point?
- **3. Don't Hold onto Past Grudges:** Bringing up past mistakes during these discussions can derail the conversation. Can you keep the focus on the present and the future?
- **4. Don't Rush:** The journey is as crucial as the destination. While it might be tempting to speed through, what would you miss along the way?

A Word of Warning:

Now, with the do's and don'ts in place, here's something to be acutely aware of: these conversations might uncover deeply rooted beliefs, past traumas, or sensitive subjects. Tread lightly. Ask yourself, is now the right time to delve deeper? Or does this topic need its own dedicated time, perhaps even with the guidance of a counselor or therapist?

Remember, this guide aims to foster understanding and connection, not to cause harm or distress. Be aware of each other's boundaries. Sometimes, it's okay to pause, take a step back, and revisit when the waters are calmer.

As you journey through these discussions, think of them as a dance. It's about rhythm, understanding, and mutual respect. At times, you lead; at other times, you follow. But always, you're in it together, moving in harmony. With these guidelines in hand, you're better equipped to ensure that this dance of conversation is graceful, enlightening, and, above all, safe.

Ready to dance?

II

Part - 2: 100 Insightful Must-Ask Questions Before Moving In With Your Partner

Part 2 of this book provides a deep dive into the critical conversations couples should have before cohabitating. These questions are designed to uncover shared values, expectations, and potential challenges, laying the foundation for a harmonious and understanding shared living experience.

Chapter 1: Financial Matters

Jason and Mia stood in the middle of their soon-to-be-shared apartment, boxes scattered around them. As Mia looked at a couch online, Jason pondered whether they needed another streaming subscription. They were diving headfirst into their new life together, and though love was in abundance, they had yet to discuss who would foot the Netflix bill or how much to set aside for their dream vacation.

Choosing "Financial Matters" as the first chapter of this journey isn't mere happenstance. When the excitement of taking the next step with your partner is fresh, discussing money might seem like a damper. Yet, countless couples, perhaps like Jason and Mia, have learned the hard way that financial clarity is fundamental to a harmonious living arrangement.

It's the unseen glue that can hold relationships together or, if mismanaged, create cracks. Imagine waking up every day in a space where there's mutual respect, not just for each other's preferences and habits but also for each other's money. This chapter aims to shed light on how couples can ensure that their shared life isn't riddled with avoidable monetary misunderstandings.

Setting financial boundaries and having a clear conversation about money early on can seem challenging, but it's a surefire way to avoid pitfalls later. Think of it as laying the first brick for your home; it determines how strong and steady the subsequent bricks—of trust, understanding, and shared dreams—will be. Discussing finances isn't about prying into each other's bank accounts; it's about understanding shared responsibilities, expectations, and goals.

From who grabs the bill at a cafe to bigger decisions like saving for a house, every penny counts in crafting a shared life. And it's not about the amount, but the intent, understanding, and transparency behind it. So before Mia and Jason proceed to fill their shared apartment with dreams, memories, and, yes, furniture, they need to sit down and hash out some crucial financial matters.

Below, you'll find ten questions that promise to guide you and your partner in building a financial foundation that's as strong as your love for each other:

1. How will we split the bills?
2. Do we have a joint bank account?
3. How much do you earn?
4. What are your monthly expenses?
5. Do you have any debts?
6. What are your savings goals?
7. How do you feel about budgeting?
8. Do you have any large upcoming expenses?
9. How will we save for big purchases?
10. Are we financially prepared for emergencies?

Take some quiet time together, maybe over a cup of coffee

or during a relaxed weekend morning, and ponder over these questions. Remember, this is a conversation, not an interrogation. Here's to crafting a future filled with mutual respect, understanding, and, of course, love.

Chapter 2: Household Responsibilities

Sam and Alex excitedly unlocked the door to their first shared apartment. With big smiles and a feeling of accomplishment, they stepped inside. The sparkle of new beginnings was in their eyes. Yet, a week later, a pile of unwashed dishes became the first silent 'tenant' of disagreement. Alex, accustomed to doing dishes right after eating, found himself perplexed by Sam's laissez-faire attitude. "It's just dishes," Sam had shrugged, not realizing the iceberg of household expectations lurking beneath.

Why "Household Responsibilities" right after financial matters, you ask?

In relationships, it's the little things that often become the big things. The mundane intricacies of daily life, like who takes out the trash or who's responsible for groceries, can sometimes evolve into matters of contention. It's these seemingly small nuances that shape the day-to-day rhythm of a couple's shared life.

While the tales of knights and princesses never told us who did the laundry in the castle, in real life, shared chores play a pivotal role. The magic isn't just in romantic dinners and surprise gifts. It's also in knowing that your partner will help clear up after a meal, or in the mutual respect of dividing household tasks. It's not about a 50-50 split; it's about understanding, adaptability, and the willingness to support each other.

Understanding each other's habits, preferences, and even pet peeves can make the journey smoother. When Sam and Alex sit down to discuss their household responsibilities, it won't just be about dishes. It'll be about understanding each other's upbringing, past living situations, and what they each see as a comfortable, functional home. Remember, it's not about pointing fingers or setting strict rules. It's about creating a harmonious living space where both feel respected and valued.

These daily tasks might seem trivial in the grand dance of love. But by discussing them, you're not only ensuring a cleaner living space but also forging a deeper bond of understanding. So before the unwashed dishes turn into a bone of contention or the laundry starts speaking the silent language of annoyance, it's wise to have a chat.

Here are ten straightforward questions to set the stage for a happy, well-organized home:

1. Who cooks?
2. Who cleans?
3. How often do we clean the house?
4. Who takes out the trash?
5. Who handles grocery shopping?
6. How often do we do laundry?
7. Do we need a chore schedule?
8. Who takes care of any pets?
9. How do we handle repairs or maintenance?
10. Do we hire help for certain tasks?

Take a cozy evening, perhaps after a shared meal (maybe even try cooking it together!), and discuss these questions. Approach them with love, understanding, and a dash of humor. After all, building a life together is as much about sharing responsibilities as it is about sharing dreams. Here's to a home filled with love, mutual respect, and teamwork!

Chapter 3: Personal Habits

In the soft glow of the morning, Emma rolled over to catch a few more minutes of sleep. The blaring alarm from Ryan's side of the bed shattered her brief moment of peace. He was an early bird, already lacing up his shoes for a morning run. Emma, a night owl, grumbled under her breath. To top it off, Ryan had a peculiar habit of leaving his socks just about everywhere, and Emma, with her love for tidiness, often found herself picking up after him. They were deeply in love, but these personal habits were slowly becoming little gremlins in their shared space.

After diving deep into financial concerns and household responsibilities, it's time to shine a light on something just as significant: personal habits. These habits, sometimes innocuous and sometimes deeply ingrained, color our everyday life. And when two people come together, it's like two different shades trying to blend on the same canvas.

Living together brings to the forefront quirks and habits that we often didn't notice while dating. Maybe it's the way one partner hums while working, or how the other leaves lights on in every room. Or perhaps it's the midnight snacking versus morning fitness routines. These habits can be endearing, amusing, or sometimes, frankly, a little annoying.

Why is it essential to address these? Because recognizing,

understanding, and navigating through these personal habits is a masterclass in patience, tolerance, and adjustment. For Emma and Ryan, it's about realizing that their differences in routines and behaviors aren't flaws but merely individualities. It's about acknowledging that what's natural for one might be alien to the other.

By discussing these habits, couples can find ways to coexist harmoniously without feeling stifled. It's not about changing who you are, but about understanding each other's rhythms, needs, and quirks. A chat over personal habits is essentially a step toward celebrating individuality while building a collective life.

As you embark on this journey of discovery and compromise, here are ten questions to help navigate the mosaic of personal habits:

1. Are you a morning person or a night owl?
2. Do you have any bedtime or morning routines?
3. What are some habits you're proud of?
4. Are there any habits you'd like to change?
5. What are some habits you think I should know about?
6. How do you wind down after a stressful day?
7. What are your eating habits like?
8. Do you smoke or drink?
9. What's your typical weekend like?
10. How do we address habits that might bother the other person?

Set aside a relaxed afternoon, perhaps in your favorite nook of the house, and dive into these questions. Keep the conversation light-hearted and judgment-free. Remember, this chat is about understanding, not criticizing. The goal is to cherish the idiosyncrasies while ensuring mutual respect. To thrive in a space where both can be unapologetically themselves, yet perfectly in tune with each other!

Chapter 4: Future Goals

As Clara and Liam sat on their balcony, watching the sunset, Clara dreamily spoke of a cottage in the countryside where they could someday retire. Liam, on the other hand, envisioned a bustling city life, even in their golden years. They both paused, realizing that while their hearts were synchronized in love, their future visions had different backdrops.

Stepping into "Future Goals" is like opening a window to the landscape of dreams, aspirations, and visions. By now, we've tackled the nitty-gritty of daily life, from finances to personal habits. But what about the horizon that extends beyond the immediate? What do you both see when you think of the future, five, ten, or even twenty years down the line?

Goals are the compass that guides life's journey. Whether it's career aspirations, dreams of travel, thoughts on family, or simply where you see yourselves living, these goals will shape the trajectory of your shared life. Discussing them isn't just about alignment; it's about understanding, supporting, and sometimes, compromising.

For Clara and Liam, it's a revelation of sorts to realize that their dreams have different settings. Yet, it's also an opportunity. An opportunity to craft a shared dream, to find a middle ground, or to figure out how they can support each other's aspirations.

Diving into future goals is also a testament to the commitment. It's a sign that you're not just thinking about the present but are genuinely invested in building a future together. It's about ensuring that as the years roll by, surprises are limited to birthdays and anniversaries, and not sudden revelations about life goals.

Let's embark on this voyage into the future with these ten guiding questions:

1. Where do you see yourself in five years? Ten years?
2. How can we help each other reach our dreams?
3. Do you have plans for further education or upskilling?
4. Where would you like to live in the long term?
5. What are your thoughts on starting a family?
6. Do you have travel goals or places you'd like to visit?
7. How do you envision your retirement?
8. Are there any personal milestones you're aiming for?
9. How do you feel about investments, like buying a house or stocks?
10. What are your aspirations in terms of health and well-being?

Maybe take an evening walk, hand in hand, or find a quiet space in your home, and let these questions be the compass guiding your conversation. As you navigate through these questions, let the undercurrent be understanding and support. Because while individual dreams are beautiful, a shared dream, woven with the threads of both aspirations, is a masterpiece. Here's to a future that's not just dreamed of but built together!

Chapter 5: Family and Friends

At a cozy dinner table, Isabelle and Aiden found themselves amidst a mild disagreement. Isabelle's family had a tradition of Sunday brunches, which she held dear. Aiden, on the other hand, valued his Saturday nights with his buddies, sometimes spilling into the wee hours of Sunday. Between family obligations and social circles, they realized the challenge of weaving together two distinct social lives.

Navigating to the chapter on "Family and Friends," we venture into the intricate tapestry of relationships that each partner brings into the union. These relationships, rich with history and emotions, play a pivotal role in the dynamics of a couple's shared life.

Every individual carries a world colored by family traditions, friendships, and social commitments. Why broach this topic after discussing personal habits and future goals? Because family and friends are an extension of one's personal history and future aspirations. They've been witnesses to past milestones and will likely play roles in future ones. It's vital to understand not just the partner you're with, but the world they come from.

For Isabelle and Aiden, it's a dance of balance. It's about honoring traditions and social commitments while ensuring they carve out their own traditions and shared social memories.

They'll need to communicate, compromise, and sometimes even stand up for their shared life when external relationships threaten their peace.

Balancing family obligations, friend commitments, and ensuring quality time as a couple can sometimes feel like juggling. But by discussing and setting boundaries, you ensure that no ball drops. More importantly, this conversation is about ensuring that external relationships enrich, not strain, the bond you're building.

Let's dive deeper into this realm of relationships with these ten guiding questions:

1. How often do we visit or host our families?
2. Are there any family traditions that are important to you?
3. How do we manage holidays and special occasions with both families?
4. What role do friends play in our life as a couple?
5. How do we handle conflicts or disagreements with family members?
6. Are there boundaries we should set with family or friends?
7. How do we integrate our separate friend groups?
8. What are your thoughts on joint social activities versus individual ones?
9. How do we prioritize our time between family, friends, and just the two of us?
10. How do we communicate and support each other during family challenges or crises?

Maybe brew a pot of tea or pour a glass of wine and settle into a comfortable spot. As you traverse these questions, let empathy and mutual respect guide the conversation. Remember, you're not just blending lives; you're blending worlds. Here's to cherishing the rich tapestry of relationships, while weaving a new one that's uniquely yours.

Chapter 6: Conflict Resolution

It was one of those evenings where a simple discussion about vacation plans turned into a heated debate between Naomi and Theo. With voices raised and words unfiltered, the room was filled with tension. Later, when the storm had passed, Naomi preferred silent reflection, while Theo sought an immediate conversation to clear the air. They were in love, yes, but they had different roadmaps for navigating disagreements.

Entering the realm of "Conflict Resolution," we touch upon a theme universal to all relationships. Every couple, no matter how compatible, will face disagreements. It's not the absence of conflict but the ability to navigate through it that strengthens a relationship's foundation.

Why place this chapter after discussing family, friends, and previous themes? Because when two people share their lives, external factors, personal habits, aspirations, and social commitments will inevitably lead to disagreements. It's essential, then, to have a strategy, a compass, if you will, to steer safely through these choppy waters.

For Naomi and Theo, the challenge lies not just in the disagreement itself but in how they both naturally respond to it. Understanding that each person has a unique way of processing emotions, seeking resolution, and healing is pivotal. It's about ensuring that in moments of conflict, they're not pulling apart but coming together.

Discussions about conflict resolution are less about preventing disagreements and more about establishing a mutual understanding of how to handle them when they arise. It's about creating a safe space where both partners feel heard, understood, and respected, even in disagreement.

Let's explore this vital territory with these ten guiding questions:

1. How do you usually react when you're upset?
2. What do you need from me when we're in disagreement?
3. How can we ensure our arguments remain respectful and productive?
4. Are there specific triggers or topics we should approach with extra care?
5. How do we address issues from the past without letting them influence current disagreements?
6. What strategies can we use to de-escalate situations?
7. Do we have a "cooling off" period when things get too heated?
8. How do we know when it's time to seek external help or counseling?
9. What are our boundaries when discussing our disagreements with friends or family?
10. How do we ensure that we're regularly checking in and addressing unresolved feelings?

Consider setting a calm and tranquil atmosphere for this conversation. Maybe light some candles or play some soft background music. As you both discuss these questions, be genuine and open, ensuring that the dialogue remains a safe space for vulnerability. Remember, it's not about who's right or wrong; it's about understanding and coming together. Here's to navigating disagreements with grace, empathy, and the assurance that every storm can lead to a brighter rainbow.

Chapter 7: Space and Privacy

Sara gazed longingly at the quaint reading nook in their shared apartment, her haven of solitude. Jake, her partner, often didn't realize her need for these silent moments of introspection. He, being the social butterfly, always loved company, often inviting friends over. While both cherished their bond, they needed to strike a balance between shared moments and individual spaces.

"Space and Privacy" leads us into a nuanced domain where we discuss the importance of individuality within a shared life. Yes, love binds people, but it's essential to recognize that each partner is still an individual with unique needs, including the need for personal space and privacy.

Why address this after diving into conflict resolution? Because respecting boundaries, understanding the need for personal space, and ensuring privacy are preventive measures that can help mitigate potential conflicts. They are cornerstones in fostering trust and mutual respect.

For Sara and Jake, the challenge lies in understanding that while love is about being together, it's also about respecting each other's boundaries. It's recognizing that solitude can be as nourishing as companionship, and that individual growth contributes to collective growth.

Ensuring space and privacy isn't about distancing. It's about providing room for self-reflection, personal hobbies, or just some downtime. It's also about ensuring that trust remains the backbone of the relationship, where neither feels surveilled or stifled.

Let's navigate this delicate balance with the following ten questions:

1. How much personal space do you need to feel comfortable and rejuvenated?
2. How do we respect each other's privacy, especially in shared living spaces?
3. What are your thoughts on personal hobbies or activities done alone?
4. How can we communicate our need for space without making the other feel excluded?
5. Do we have boundaries when it comes to personal gadgets and social media?
6. How do we balance group activities with friends and personal time?
7. What are your thoughts on individual retreats or solo vacations?
8. How can we ensure that our personal spaces, like desks or closets, are respected?
9. Do you have any privacy concerns that I should be aware of?
10. How do we check-in to ensure that our needs for space and privacy evolve and are understood?

Perhaps pick a serene evening, maybe by the window or in your shared living space, to discuss these questions. Maintain a gentle, understanding tone, ensuring that it's a conversation of love and respect. Remember, a relationship is not only about coming together but also about letting each other breathe. Here's to celebrating togetherness while cherishing individuality.

Chapter 8: Communication

On their date night, Rachel scribbled something on a napkin and slid it over to Tom. It read, "How's your heart today?" It was their little ritual, a simple question that invited deep conversations. Tom appreciated these moments. For him, words often got tangled up, but with Rachel's patient nudges, he learned to untangle them.

"Communication" is the bridge that connects all aspects of a relationship. From understanding needs and desires to expressing discomforts and joys, communication is the very foundation upon which relationships are built and nurtured.

Why focus on this after discussing space and privacy? Because effective communication is what makes the balance between togetherness and individuality seamless. It's the tool through which partners express their need for space, articulate boundaries, and share dreams and fears.

For Rachel and Tom, it's about creating a safe space for expression. Rachel's simple gesture of asking about Tom's heart is her way of inviting open dialogue. For Tom, it's about learning that communication isn't just about speaking but also about being heard and understood.

Communication in a relationship isn't just about daily updates or planning the next vacation. It's also about discussing fears, aspirations, vulnerabilities, and joys. It's about ensuring that the bond remains strong, not just in moments of love but also in moments of misunderstanding.

Dive into this realm of shared words and unspoken feelings with these ten questions:

1. How do you prefer to communicate difficult emotions or topics?
2. How can we ensure that our communication remains open and non-judgmental?
3. What are some signals or signs we can develop for when one of us needs to talk?
4. How do we approach topics that we've historically avoided or tiptoed around?
5. What role does non-verbal communication play in our relationship?
6. How do we ensure that both of us feel equally heard in conversations?
7. Are there any words, phrases, or tones that we should be cautious about using?
8. How do we create a safe space for sharing vulnerabilities and insecurities?
9. How do we address misunderstandings or miscommunications?
10. How frequently should we have deep, heart-to-heart conversations?

Consider setting aside dedicated time for this conversation. Maybe during a quiet evening or a relaxed weekend morning. As you both explore these questions, let authenticity and genuine curiosity guide the conversation. Remember, in the world of relationships, communication is the melody that makes the dance of love harmonious. Here's to speaking, listening, understanding, and growing together.

Chapter 9: Shared Activities

Amidst the laughter and cheers of the bowling alley, Layla and Marco discovered something new about their relationship. Marco, with his competitive spirit, aimed for a strike every time, while Layla was just in it for the fun, celebrating every small win. They realized that their shared activities weren't just about the activity itself but about the joy, challenges, and learnings they brought to their bond.

"Shared Activities" takes us on a delightful journey into the world of shared hobbies, interests, and pastimes. Engaging in activities together not only strengthens the bond between partners but also helps create a reservoir of shared memories.

But why emphasize shared activities after discussing communication? Because these activities often serve as avenues for non-verbal communication, for understanding each other's personalities, and for bonding without the need for words.

For Layla and Marco, their bowling alley escapades weren't just about the game. It was about understanding each other's temperaments, celebrating each other's wins, and learning how to cheer each other on even when we missed. Shared activities aren't just about doing something together; they're about experiencing, understanding, and growing together.

Embarking on shared hobbies, be they cooking, hiking, dancing, or even just watching movies, infuses the relationship with fun and intimacy. But, it's equally essential to ensure these activities align with both partners' interests and comfort levels.

Let's roll into the fun world of shared pastimes with these ten guiding questions:

1. What activities do you currently love doing together?
2. Are there any new hobbies or interests you'd like to explore as a couple?
3. How do we ensure our shared activities cater to both our interests?
4. Are there activities we used to enjoy together but have stopped? Why?
5. How do we balance competitive and casual, relaxed activities?
6. How frequently should we engage in these shared activities?
7. How do we handle situations where one of us isn't as interested or enthusiastic about a particular activity?
8. Are there activities that either of us would like to reserve as 'me-time'?
9. How can we encourage and support each other in these shared pursuits?
10. How do we ensure we're continuously introducing novelty and keeping the excitement alive in our shared activities?

Plan a light-hearted evening, perhaps over a shared meal or amidst nature, to discuss these questions. As you explore these questions, let enthusiasm and mutual respect be your guiding lights. Remember, it's not about the score, but the game; it's not about the destination, but the journey. Here's to crafting memories, laughs, and moments that will become cherished stories in the annals of your relationship.

Chapter 10: Intimacy and Affection

Under the soft glow of the fairy lights in their backyard, Zoe and Adrian swayed gently to their favorite song. It was their way of reconnecting after a busy week. Those silent moments of closeness, the warmth of a hand-held, or a kiss on the forehead, spoke volumes. For them, intimacy wasn't just about passionate moments, but also the quiet reassurances and gestures of love.

"Intimacy and Affection" delicately unfolds the layers of physical and emotional closeness in a relationship. These are the threads that not only bind hearts but also allow partners to feel seen, cherished, and truly understood.

Why discuss intimacy after shared activities? Because while shared hobbies bring fun and bonding, intimacy cements the emotional connection. It is through moments of affection and closeness that partners reassure each other of their love, commitment, and presence in each other's lives.

For Zoe and Adrian, intimacy isn't always about grand gestures. Sometimes, it's the silent dance in their backyard, or the way they instinctively reach out for each other's hands when walking. Intimacy is as much about the unspoken feelings as it is about the physical connection.

In a world where days rush by, ensuring moments of intimacy and affection becomes paramount. It's about ensuring that amidst the noise, there's always a silent sanctuary of connection and understanding.

Dive deep into this world of heartbeats and soft touches with these ten insightful questions:

1. How do you define intimacy in our relationship?
2. What are the gestures or moments that make you feel most connected and loved?
3. How can we ensure we're prioritizing intimacy, especially during busy or stressful times?
4. Are there boundaries or comfort levels we need to discuss regarding physical intimacy?
5. How do you feel about public displays of affection?
6. What role does verbal affirmation play in our intimacy?
7. Are there any past experiences or insecurities we should be aware of to better understand each other's intimacy needs?
8. How do we address moments when our intimacy needs might not align?
9. How can we explore and enhance our emotional intimacy?
10. How frequently should we check in on our intimacy and affection needs to ensure we're both fulfilled?

Choose a comfortable and intimate setting, maybe by candlelight or during a peaceful morning, to explore these questions together. As you navigate this chapter, approach it with the utmost respect, sensitivity, and open-heartedness. Remember, intimacy is the silent song of the soul, the gentle touch that says, "I'm here, with you, always." Here's to the whispers, the soft touches, and the heartbeats that synchronize in love.

Chapter 11: Health and Medical conditions

Under the soft glow of the room's lamp, Maya gently applied the ointment to Alex's eczema flare-up. While it wasn't a life-threatening condition, it did require attention and understanding. Maya remembered the early days when Alex felt self-conscious about it. Over time, with open conversations and trust, they tackled not only Alex's skin issues but also navigated the deeper waters of their health histories and concerns.

"Health and Medical Conditions" delves deep into the personal realm of our physical well-being, vulnerabilities, and the inevitable ups and downs of health that life brings. These topics, though delicate, are critical in ensuring that partners stand as pillars of strength for each other.

Why address health after discussing pets? Because, akin to the long-term commitment of pet ownership, understanding and supporting a partner's health is an enduring pledge. It's about being there in sickness and in health, literally.

For Maya and Alex, it's more than just dealing with a skin condition. It's about vulnerability, trust, and the commitment to face health challenges together. It's about understanding that while love is the foundation, knowledge and empathy toward each other's health conditions provide stability.

Navigating through health issues is a testament to the depth of understanding, patience, and resilience of a partnership.

Embark on this sensitive journey with these ten poignant questions:

1. Are there any current medical conditions or health concerns you'd like me to be aware of?
2. How can we best support each other during health-related challenges?
3. Do we have a clear understanding of each other's medical histories?
4. How do we approach the topic of mental health and ensure we're there for each other?
5. What are our stances on regular medical check-ups and preventive healthcare?
6. How do we handle situations where one of us is temporarily incapacitated or needs extended care?
7. Are there any genetic or hereditary conditions in your family that I should know about?
8. How do we communicate our needs during times when we're feeling ill or under medical stress?
9. What are our health-related boundaries, especially concerning privacy or personal care?
10. How do we ensure we're both equipped with knowledge and resources in case of emergencies?

Choose a serene environment, perhaps over a calming cup of tea or during a tranquil evening, to discuss these questions. When navigating this chapter, approach it with compassion, an open heart, and the understanding that health forms the very core of

CHAPTER 11: HEALTH AND MEDICAL CONDITIONS

our existence. Here's to being the sanctuary of comfort, trust, and unwavering support for each other in both the sunny and stormy days of health.

Chapter 12: Career Conversations

As Ryan meticulously adjusted his tie, staring into the mirror, the weight of the upcoming job interview was evident in his eyes. Beside him, Lara offered a reassuring squeeze to his hand. They had discussed this job change at length, understanding the implications for their shared life, the possible relocations, and the changes in routines. This wasn't just Ryan's career move; it was a step forward in their shared journey.

"Career Conversations" shines a spotlight on the ambitions, aspirations, and decisions that propel us forward in our professional lives. Yet, these aren't solo ventures, especially when in a committed relationship. Every promotion, job change, or even a challenging project can ripple into our shared lives.

After diving deep into health matters, why pivot to Careers? Because, in the grand tapestry of life, career decisions, much like health, play a pivotal role in shaping daily routines, life choices, and even our self-worth.

For Lara and Ryan, it's not just about a job change. It's about dreams, aspirations, and the sacrifices or adjustments they might have to make together. It's about celebrating victories and navigating through setbacks, hand in hand.

Professional aspirations are intertwined with personal dreams, and understanding them is key to a harmonious life together.

Ponder over these ten instrumental questions:

1. How do you envision your career trajectory in the next 5-10 years?
2. What are your biggest professional aspirations, and how can I support you in achieving them?
3. How do we handle potential relocations or long-distance phases due to career choices?
4. How do we ensure work stresses don't spill into our personal lives?
5. How do we approach decisions that might involve significant changes in work-life balance?
6. What are our expectations when it comes to work-related social events or commitments?
7. How can we best communicate during busy or high-pressure periods at work?
8. How do we support each other during career transitions or uncertainties?
9. Are there any professional dreams or aspirations you haven't shared with me yet?
10. How can we ensure that our individual career goals align with our collective dreams and plans?

Sit down, perhaps after a workday or during a relaxed weekend morning, to converse about these questions. When diving into this chapter, bring along a spirit of mutual respect, encouragement, and the understanding that career journeys aren't just about individual growth but about growing together. Here's to shared dreams, compromises, and the joy of seeing each other achieve and thrive in the professional realm.

Chapter 13: Overnight Guests

Amelia's heart raced as she heard the doorbell. Her college friend, Megan, was visiting for the weekend. Amelia was ecstatic, but she also remembered that Jason, her partner, was a bit apprehensive about having guests over, especially for extended stays. Their apartment was their shared sanctuary, and Amelia knew the importance of addressing Jason's concerns while welcoming her friend.

"Overnight Guests" dives into the dynamics of opening your shared living space to friends, family, or acquaintances. A home, after all, isn't just a structure of bricks and mortar; it's a personal space, filled with routines, comforts, and private moments.

But why tackle this after a chapter on intimacy? Because while intimacy is about connecting with your partner, accommodating guests is about broadening that sphere of connection and understanding. It's about navigating shared spaces, boundaries, and the comforts of home with others in the picture.

For Amelia and Jason, it's a lesson in balancing hospitality with personal space. While Amelia thrives in the company of old friends, Jason treasures the sanctity of their shared home. Their challenge is to ensure guests feel welcome without overshadowing their shared routines and boundaries.

CHAPTER 13: OVERNIGHT GUESTS

Entertaining guests, especially overnight ones, is about ensuring mutual respect and understanding between partners while extending warmth and hospitality to visitors.

Let's understand this dynamic better with these ten questions:

1. How do you feel about having overnight guests in our home?
2. What kind of notice or heads-up would you prefer before someone stays over?
3. Are there specific boundaries or house rules we should communicate to our guests?
4. How do we ensure our routines, especially private or intimate moments, aren't disrupted with guests around?
5. How frequently is it comfortable for us to host overnight guests?
6. Are there specific people you'd be more or less comfortable having as an overnight guest?
7. How can we ensure both of us are on the same page regarding entertaining and hosting responsibilities?
8. What are our expectations for each other when either of us invites someone over?
9. How do we address potential conflicts or disagreements about guests?
10. How can we ensure that both our comfort levels and needs are considered when opening our home to others?

Take some time, perhaps over a quiet dinner or while lounging together, to address these questions. As you navigate through them, prioritize mutual understanding and respect. Remember, a home is both a personal sanctuary and a place of shared memories. Here's to creating a space that's welcoming yet retains its essence of comfort and intimacy for the two of you.

Chapter 14: Pets

Samantha gazed lovingly at the little bundle of fur nestled in her lap, purring contentedly. She had always been a cat person, cherishing the quiet companionship cats offered. However, her partner, Derek, had grown up with boisterous dogs and longed for the playful energy they brought. As they contemplated expanding their fur family, they realized it was more than just picking a pet—it was about blending their histories, preferences, and future plans.

"Pets" introduces us to the world of furry, feathery, or even scaly companions that often become integral parts of our families. These beloved creatures bring joy, responsibility, and a unique dynamic to any household.

After discussing guests, why dive into pets? Because, like guests, pets become a part of your shared environment. However, unlike temporary guests, pets are a long-term commitment, impacting daily routines, plans, and even vacations.

For Samantha and Derek, it's not just about deciding between a cat or a dog. It's about understanding what each pet means to them, the memories associated with them, and the shared responsibility they'll undertake.

Pets, in many ways, become a testament to a couple's ability to care, compromise, and co-parent. Whether it's feeding, training, or cuddling, pets require a joint effort.

Leap into this world of wagging tails, soft purrs, and shared responsibilities with these ten thought-provoking questions:

1. How do you feel about having pets in our shared home?
2. Which pets do you have a preference for, and why?
3. Are there any pets you're uncomfortable with or allergic to?
4. How do we distribute pet-related responsibilities such as feeding, walking, or vet visits?
5. How do we approach the financial responsibilities that come with pet ownership?
6. What's our stance on training, disciplining, or setting boundaries for our pets?
7. How will our pet's presence influence our travel or vacation plans?
8. In the case of potential moves or relocations, how do we ensure our pet's well-being?
9. What happens if one of us becomes more attached to or bonded with the pet?
10. How do we handle potential disagreements about pet care or decisions?

Choose a cozy spot, perhaps with a pet if you already have one, or while taking a stroll in a park watching pets play, to discuss these questions. As you dive into this chapter, let empathy, foresight, and mutual understanding guide you. Remember, pets are not just additions to your home; they become family. Here's to the shared joys, challenges, and unforgettable moments that pets can bring into your lives together.

Chapter 15: Breaking Up and Moving Out

The coffee shop was filled with a soft hum of chatter, but for Zoe and Max, the world seemed to have narrowed down to just their table. Their hands clasped together, tears forming in their eyes. They loved each other immensely, but certain irreconcilable differences meant they had to part ways. This wasn't a hasty decision but one born from countless conversations, understanding, and the realization that sometimes, love alone isn't enough.

"Breaking Up" might seem like an odd topic in a guide about moving in together. Yet, it's a vital discussion. Relationships, despite all the love and effort, sometimes reach a point where the healthiest and kindest option is to part ways.

Why venture into this after a chapter on career aspirations? Because, while careers talk about building and looking ahead, this chapter is a reminder that not all paths, no matter how carefully planned, lead to the destinations we envision.

For Zoe and Max, it's about understanding that breaking up doesn't diminish their past love or the memories they created. It's about recognizing that love, though powerful, is sometimes not enough to bridge certain gaps or differences.

Breakups aren't failures; they're acknowledgments of the

need for different paths to personal growth and happiness.

Reflect on these ten somber yet essential questions:

1. If we decide to part ways, how can we do it respectfully and clearly?
2. How will we manage shared money or things if we break up?
3. What's the best way for us to talk if one of us thinks about ending the relationship?
4. Should we consider relationship counseling if we face big challenges?
5. If we break up, how do we sort out our shared living space and things?
6. How will we handle our shared friends or events if we separate?
7. How can we help each other emotionally if we decide to end things?
8. After breaking up, what should our contact with each other look like?
9. What do we do with shared memories or items if we split?
10. If we end our relationship, how can we ensure it leads to personal growth and not resentment?

Take a moment, maybe in a quiet setting or during a heartfelt conversation, to discuss these questions. While it might be challenging, it's essential to remember that this chapter isn't about anticipating an end but about understanding that every relationship's ultimate goal is the well-being and happiness of the individuals involved. Here's to hoping that every ending paves the way for new beginnings, filled with lessons, love, and an enduring respect for the journey shared.

Conclusion: The Journey Continues...

As the final words of this guide meet your eyes, it's essential to remember that the last page doesn't signal the end but the beginning of a profound journey. Embarking on the shared voyage of understanding and commitment with your partner is an ongoing process that will be filled with moments of clarity, discovery, and deepening bonds.

Your decision to invest in this book—and more importantly, in your relationship—is commendable. Every question you've pondered, every conversation you've initiated, and every understanding you've reached are the stepping stones to a richer, more harmonious life together. For taking that step, for choosing love, understanding, and growth, a heartfelt *thank you*.

If this guide has been a compass for your relationship's journey, would you consider sharing your experiences? Reviews do more than just provide feedback—they light the way for others. Think of the countless couples out there, standing on the precipice of this very journey, seeking guidance and assurance. Your insights could be the beacon they need. Your shared experiences, your revelations, and even your challenges can offer them invaluable insights.

By leaving a review, you're not just helping me refine and evolve this guide for future editions, but you're also extending a hand to those searching for clarity and connection in their relationships. A few moments of your time can ripple out, creating a positive impact for countless others.

In a world increasingly driven by fleeting moments and instant gratifications, championing deeper connections, mutual understanding, and genuine commitment is ever so crucial. By sharing your review, you contribute to a larger narrative—one of love, patience, and growth.

In essence, your journey, your story, and your voice matter. Let it resonate, let it guide, and let it inspire.

Once again, thank you for joining me on this voyage. Wishing you endless moments of discovery, joy, and love. And as you navigate the intricate dance of togetherness, remember: the best tunes are yet to be played, and the finest steps are yet to be danced.

Warmly,

Yakalou

III

Part - 3: Bonus Chapters

"Bonus Chapters" delves into comprehensive guides and checklists, ensuring you're thoroughly prepared for every phase of your moving journey, from pre-move planning to settling in. It also offers profound introspection on financial and personal considerations, equipping you with the tools and insights needed for a smooth transition and harmonious cohabitation.

The Moving Checklist: From 8 Weeks Before to 4 Weeks After

The Ultimate Moving Checklist: From 8 Weeks Before to 4 Weeks After

Leila and Max sat in a room filled with scattered belongings. A ticking clock reminded them of the fast-approaching moving day. Max, ever the planner, pulled out a worn notebook. Scribbled on its pages was a meticulously planned checklist. Each step, from 8 weeks before the move to 4 weeks after, was detailed. They sighed in relief; this checklist was their roadmap through the chaos.

"The Ultimate Moving Checklist" is your lifeboat in the tempestuous sea of relocating. Relocating your lives together is no small feat. There are a myriad of emotions, from excitement to anxiety. What furnishings do we bring? What gets left behind? How do we ensure we don't misplace the essentials?

Placing this chapter after discussing intimacy might seem out of place, but here's the beauty: while previous chapters addressed the emotional aspects of moving in, this one is about the tangible, practical steps. It's about setting the stage for all the love and shared moments to come.

Max's foresight in crafting that checklist for him and Leila wasn't just about organization. It symbolized his commitment to ensuring their shared journey was smooth. Now, let's help you pave your path with a similar intention.

8 Weeks Before:

1. Begin decluttering room by room.
2. Create an inventory list of major items.
3. Research and select a reputable moving company.
4. Get moving supplies: boxes, bubble wrap, markers, etc.
5. Start packing rarely used items.
6. Confirm the moving date and schedule time off work if necessary.
7. Notify important institutions (banks, post offices, etc.) about the impending move.
8. Start a 'moving folder' for all related paperwork.
9. Prioritize items based on necessity.
10. Begin exploring utilities and service providers in your new location.

6 Weeks Before:

11. Continue packing, labeling boxes by room and content.
12. Separate valuables and essential documents.
13. Make a list of people to notify about the move.
14. Begin researching address change requirements.
15. Clear out any rented storage units or lockers.
16. Plan for pet and plant relocations.
17. Begin consuming perishables to reduce waste on moving day.

18. Start disassembling rarely used furniture.
19. Consider a garage sale or donations for unwanted items.
20. Secure the moving company's services.

4 Weeks Before:

21. Increase packing pace, keeping daily necessities accessible.
22. Confirm the transfer of utilities.
23. Notify doctors, schools, etc. of the move.
24. Begin collecting medical records and important documents.
25. Reconfirm the moving date.
26. Finalize the 'moving day' plan.
27. Update addresses for subscriptions and memberships.
28. Ensure enough cash is on hand for moving day emergencies.
29. Check for necessary parking permits or special requirements.
30. Pack a 'first day' box with essentials.

2 Weeks Before:

31. Double-check your inventory list.
32. Finish packing, except for daily essentials.
33. Disassemble the remaining furniture.
34. Confirm the new address details with the moving company.
35. Update the address with the post office.
36. Clean or schedule cleaning for the current residence.
37. Confirm the setup of utilities for the new home.
38. Create a move-day itinerary.

39. Arrange for childcare or pet care on moving day, if necessary.
40. Check in with the moving company one last time.

Moving Week:

41. Pack daily essentials, clothes for the next few days.
42. Defrost the refrigerator.
43. Reconfirm the arrival time of the movers.
44. Gather all keys, remotes, etc., to hand over or take.
45. Dispose of any final trash.
46. Pack the 'first night' box in an accessible place.
47. Settle any remaining bills.
48. Do a final walk-through of the home.
49. Keep personal valuables separate when transporting yourself.
50. Rest well the night before.

Moving Day:

51. Be available for any mover's questions.
52. Protect floors and corners from moving damage.
53. Do a final sweep once the movers finish.
54. Ensure the movers have the correct new address.
55. Lock up your old home.
56. Read meters before leaving.
57. Travel to the new home.
58. Supervise the unloading process.
59. Begin unpacking the essentials.
60. Take a deep breath—you've moved!

2 Weeks After:

61. Start unpacking systematically, room by room.
62. Check all items against your inventory.
63. Notify friends and family of the successful move.
64. Begin exploring the neighborhood.
65. Register with local essential services (like doctors, vets).
66. Share your new address with your contact list.
67. Get any necessary new licenses or IDs.
68. Begin setting up utilities and services.
69. Send out thank-you notes if you received moving help.
70. Start re-establishing daily routines.

4 Weeks After:

71. Finish any remaining unpacking.
72. Purchase any additional furniture or household items.
73. Check in with the post office to ensure mail is arriving.
74. Begin establishing local connections: clubs, activities, etc.
75. Give feedback to your moving company.
76. Store all moving paperwork in a safe place.
77. Host a housewarming (if desired).
78. Reflect on the moving process for future reference.
79. Ensure all old bills and obligations are settled.
80. Bask in your new shared home!

Now, post-move, ponder over these questions:

1. What aspects of the move did we handle particularly well as a team?
2. Were there elements we overlooked in our moving checklist?
3. What were our most significant challenges during this move?
4. How did our communication aid (or hinder) the moving process?
5. How did we handle stress or unexpected issues that arose?
6. Were there any surprises about our possessions or what we deemed necessary?
7. How can we better prepare for any future relocations?
8. How do we feel in our new space?
9. What's the first shared memory we want to create here?
10. Looking back, what's the most valuable lesson from this move?

Take a moment, amidst the boxes and new surroundings, to reflect. Moving in together is more than just merging spaces; it's intertwining lives. May your new abode be filled with love, laughter, and countless shared moments.

The 50 Must-Have Essentials & Tools Before Moving In

Amara's eyes widened as she tried to use a butter knife to unscrew a bolt. Nearby, Tom was attempting to open a box with his car keys. They laughed at their mismatched tools and shared an exasperated look. It was apparent that amidst the whirlwind of moving, they had overlooked one crucial thing: the tools and essentials they'd need for setting up their new home together.

Ensuring you have the right tools and essentials can make the difference between a smooth move and an exasperating one. After the chaos of moving day, the last thing you need is the frustration of not having a can opener for your dinner or lacking the correct screwdriver to assemble your bed. This chapter isn't just about objects; it's about foresight, preparation, and creating a space that feels truly like home from day one.

Amara and Tom's playful predicament underscores an essential point: as crucial as it is to decide what you're bringing to your new home, it's equally vital to ensure you have the tools to make those belongings functional.

Kitchen Essentials:

1. Pots and pans (at least one large pot, one frying pan).
2. Basic utensils (spoons, forks, knives).
3. Plates, bowls, and glasses.
4. Can opener.
5. Measuring cups and spoons.
6. Baking dishes (for oven use).
7. Toaster or toaster oven.
8. Microwave.
9. Coffee maker or kettle.
10. Trash bags and trash cans.

Bedroom Basics:

11. Bedframe and mattress.
12. Bedding (sheets, pillows, comforters).
13. Curtains or blinds for privacy.
14. Clothes hangers.
15. Nightstands or bedside tables.
16. Alarm clock.
17. Lamps.
18. Under-bed storage bins.
19. Mirror.
20. Dresser or wardrobe.

Bathroom Necessities:

21. Towels (bath and hand).
22. Toilet paper.
23. Shower curtain and rings.

24. Bath mat.
25. Toothbrush and toothpaste.
26. Shampoo and soap.
27. Plunger and toilet brush.
28. Trash can.
29. Basic first aid kit.
30. Hairdryer.

Toolbox Must-Haves:

31. Hammer.
32. Screwdriver set (Phillips and flat-head).
33. Measuring tape.
34. Pliers.
35. Utility knife.
36. Wrench set.
37. Nails, screws, and wall anchors.
38. Flashlight or headlamp.
39. Drill (with various bits).
40. Ladder or step stool.

Miscellaneous Essentials:

41. Cleaning supplies (broom, mop, cleaning cloths).
42. Laundry detergent and basket.
43. Dish soap and sponges.
44. Extension cords and power strips.
45. Light bulbs.
46. Batteries.
47. Notepad and pen.

48. Stapler and scissors.
49. Duct tape.
50. Candles and matches (for emergencies).

And now, as you scan your space filled with boxes, bags, and scattered memories, reflect on these 10 questions:

1. Which of the above essentials had we overlooked, and how did we manage without them?
2. Are there any unique or specific tools we found we needed based on our items or new home?
3. How did preparing (or not preparing) with these essentials influence our first few days of moving in?
4. Were there any items we regretted not having on hand immediately?
5. Did we discover any redundancies – things both of us brought that we didn't need two of?
6. Which items made our transition into our new home smoother?
7. Are there any region-specific items we need due to our new location's climate or layout?
8. Were there any surprise purchases or last-minute store runs?
9. How did we decide on the brand or quality of these essentials?
10. Looking forward, are there other essentials we anticipate needing in the next few months?

From this moment on, every tool you use, every plate you set down, and every light you switch on becomes a piece of the mosaic of your shared life. Ensure you have the right pieces, not just for functionality but for creating countless memories together.

The 100 Must-Have Items You Need After Moving In

Rosa stood amidst a sea of boxes, her excitement waning as the magnitude of the task ahead became apparent. "I can't believe we forgot to pack our cutlery," she mused aloud, opening a takeout box with chopsticks she found in a drawer. Nearby, Jackson held up a single mismatched sock. "And we might need to stock up on more of these," he chuckled.

Now that you've settled into your new place, the real challenge begins: making it a comfortable, functional, and truly *homey* space. This chapter takes you beyond the initial hurdles of moving and into the nuances of everyday living. It's about optimizing your shared space, from safety precautions to homely comforts.

Remember Rosa and Jackson? They discovered that even with the most thorough pre-move planning, there's always something that gets overlooked or becomes a need only once you're living in the space. So, whether you're trying to find your footing in the kitchen, making your living space cozy, or prepping for unexpected challenges, this checklist is designed to ensure you're well-equipped.

Kitchen and Dining Add-ons:

1. Spice rack with basic spices.
2. Blender or food processor.
3. Dish drying rack.
4. Baking sheets and muffin tins.
5. Glass storage containers.
6. Wine glasses and corkscrew.
7. Ice cube trays.
8. Mixing bowls.
9. Grater and peeler.
10. Oven mitts and pot holders.

Living Room Luxuries:

11. Cozy throw blankets.
12. Decorative cushions.
13. Bookshelves or wall-mounted shelves.
14. Rugs or carpets.
15. Television and remote.
16. Streaming device or DVD player.
17. Indoor plants.
18. Picture frames and wall art.
19. Floor or table lamps.
20. Candles and holders.

Bedroom Enhancements:

21. Extra pillowcases and bed sheets.
22. Wardrobe organizers.
23. Jewelry organizer.

24. Humidifier or dehumidifier.
25. Sleep masks and earplugs.
26. A white noise machine.
27. Decorative wall hooks.
28. Shoe rack or organizer.
29. Laundry hamper with lid.
30. Mood lighting options.

Bathroom Boosters:

31. Extra hand towels and washcloths.
32. Facial tissue.
33. Bathrobe and slippers.
34. Electric toothbrush and replacement heads.
35. Shower caddy.
36. Bath bombs or salts.
37. Body lotion and hand cream.
38. Extra toiletries for guests.
39. Aromatherapy oils or diffuser.
40. Cosmetic organizers.

Safety and Maintenance:

41. Smoke and carbon monoxide detectors.
42. First-aid enhancements (burn cream, heat/cold packs).
43. Tool enhancements (Stud finder, adjustable wrench).
44. Home security system or camera.
45. Fire extinguisher.
46. Safety locks for windows.
47. Spare light bulbs and fuses.
48. Weatherstripping or insulation kits.

49. Pest control supplies.
50. Water filters or purifiers.

Outdoor and Balcony Bliss:

51. Patio or balcony furniture.
52. Grill or barbecue essentials.
53. Garden tools (if applicable).
54. Outdoor lighting.
55. Bird feeder or bird bath.
56. Plant pots and soil.
57. Hammock or swing chair.
58. Umbrella or shade.
59. Outdoor rugs.
60. Gardening gloves and knee pads.

Office or Study Staples:

61. Ergonomic chair and desk.
62. Laptop stand or docking station.
63. Printer and cartridges.
64. Noticeboard or corkboard.
65. Desk organizers.
66. Shredder.
67. Backup drive or cloud storage.
68. Comfortable headphones or earbuds.
69. Stationery (stapler, pens, highlighters).
70. Calendar or planner.

Entertainment and Leisure:

71. Board games or card games.
72. Music system or speakers.
73. Portable projector.
74. Craft supplies or hobby kits.
75. Puzzles or brain games.
76. Magazine subscriptions.
77. Yoga mats or exercise equipment.
78. Novels or coffee table books.
79. Musical instruments.
80. VR headset or gaming console.

Guest Room Graces:

81. Spare bedding sets.
82. Reading materials.
83. Universal phone charger.
84. Travel-sized toiletries.
85. Guestbook or welcome note.
86. Night light.
87. Spare slippers.
88. Empty hangers and drawer space.
89. Local guidebook or maps.
90. Snack basket or mini-fridge.

Miscellaneous Marvels:

91. Multi-purpose cleaner.
92. Wall-mounted key holder.
93. Collapsible step stool.

94. Reusable grocery bags.
95. Pet supplies (if you have or plan to have pets).
96. Sewing kit.
97. Air purifiers or fans.
98. Vacuum cleaner or robo-vac.
99. Wireless charging pads.
100. Voice-assistant device.

As you continue to adjust and flourish in your new shared space, it's essential to reflect:

1. Which items on this list do we already own, and which do we need to purchase?
2. How will these tools enhance our daily living experience?
3. Which items will foster a sense of community in our new home?
4. How can we prioritize sustainability in our purchases?
5. How do we maintain a balance between necessities and luxuries?
6. Are there items we had never considered but now find essential?
7. How does our space influence the items we choose?
8. What personal touches can we add to make our home uniquely ours?
9. How do we ensure our home stays clutter-free while accommodating these essentials?
10. In a year, which items do we anticipate will have added the most value to our lives?

A home isn't just walls and a roof; it's a living, evolving entity molded by those who inhabit it. This chapter is more than just a list; it's a nudge toward creating a space filled with love, convenience, and cherished moments.

120 Money Questions To Understand Each Other Financial Mindset

Money, as they say, makes the world go 'round. Yet, it's not just about the numbers, the bank balances, or the crisp notes in our wallets. Money is deeply intertwined with our values, our dreams, our fears, and our histories. It's a reflection of our past decisions, our current priorities, and our future aspirations. When it comes to relationships, especially the significant step of moving in with a partner, money can either be a bridge or a barrier.

The decision to share a home is more than just a romantic gesture; it's a merging of lives, and often, a merging of finances. It's about sharing costs, responsibilities, and dreams. But before you take that step, it's crucial to understand not just your own financial beliefs and habits, but also those of your partner.

"Deep Money Questions" is not just a list; it's a journey. A journey of introspection, understanding, and alignment. These 120 questions are designed to help you gain clarity about your financial life and that of your partner. They will prompt discussions about spending habits, financial goals, debts, and dreams. Some questions might be easy to answer, while others might require deep reflection. But each one is essential in its own right.

By the end of this chapter, you'll not only have a clearer picture of where you stand financially, but you'll also be better equipped to navigate the financial intricacies of cohabitation. So, take a deep breath, grab a pen, and let's dive into the depths of your financial psyche. Your future self, and perhaps your future shared life, will thank you for it.

1. How would you describe the area you grew up in, fancy, modest, or else?
2. Did your family talk about money together when you were growing up?
3. Did both of your parents work?
4. Were you aware of how much money your parents made when you were a child?
5. Do you think your parents did a good job managing their money?
6. Is there anything you would change about how your parents dealt with money while you were a child?
7. Did your parents discuss family financial matters with you?
8. Did your parents buy you everything you wanted or tell you when they couldn't afford something?
9. Do your parents pay for any of your current bills?
10. What did you learn about money from your parents? And which of these beliefs have you adopted as your own?
11. What scares you about money?
12. Do you have any bad memories from growing up that are associated with money?
13. What do you wish you knew about money when you were growing up that you know now?
14. Did you get an allowance as a kid? If yes, what did you do with it?

15. Would you give money to your siblings if they were in a difficult financial situation? Would you seek repayment?
16. Would you accept financial help from your friends or relatives?
17. Did your family go on vacations when you were young? Where did you go?
18. Have you taken any fun vacations recently?
19. Do you have any more vacations planned or any dream vacations?
20. What do you tend to splurge on?
21. What's one splurge you will never give up?
22. What was the last big thing you bought? Was it worth it?
23. Would you rather spend money on experiences or things?
24. If money was no object, what is one thing you have always dreamed of doing or buying?
25. What does having money mean to you?
26. What does being good with money mean to you?
27. What's the biggest money mistake you've made?
28. What's the best financial lesson you have learned so far?
29. What would it take for you to be happy about your financial situation?
30. How far ahead do you usually plan financially?
31. Where do you see yourself in 5, 10, and 15 years?
32. Are you currently saving for anything?
33. If you won the lottery tomorrow, what are the first three things you would spend the money on?
34. Do you financially support anyone else?
35. What do you do for work?
36. What do you want to do with your career? What's your dream job?
37. How much do you make?

38. Do you believe you are being paid fairly at your job?
39. Are there ways to increase your income?
40. Do you plan on staying in the same job, or will you look for a new job sometime in the future?
41. Do you want to pay for more education in the future?
42. Do you pay alimony or child support?
43. Do you want kids / or more?
44. When we have children, will we both continue working? Will one of us stay home with the kids? If so, who will stay home and who will work?
45. If we had children, would we send them to public or private schools?
46. Will we be saving for our children's college education?
47. Should our kids get a regular allowance? How much?
48. When you get a little extra money, what do you usually do with it? Spend it or save it?
49. Are you a spender or a saver?
50. Do you have any money saved?
51. Have you tried to reduce your spending before to save?
52. What steps do you take to save money when you needed?
53. How much do you want to save for emergencies?
54. How do you feel about debt?
55. Do you believe there is good and bad debt?
56. Do you owe any money to friends or family?
57. How much debt do you have?
58. Do you have debt that I'm not aware of?
59. If you have debt, how are you taking care of it?
60. (If you're paying off debt): What do you think about your progress so far?
61. How much do you spend on interest payments each month?
62. (If you're paying off debt): Should you change anything

about your debt repayment plan?
63. Do you prefer buying things with cash or credit?
64. Do you want to create a prenuptial agreement?
65. How much do we want to spend on a wedding?
66. How do we plan on paying for our wedding?
67. Where do we want to go on a honeymoon?
68. What would you like our life to look like in 10 years financially?
69. Do you know where we stand financially?
70. What are our short-term financial goals?
71. What are our long-term financial goals?
72. Do you feel like we're on track financially to achieve our goals?
73. Who will manage the long-term finances for the family?
74. Who will manage the family's finances day to day?
75. How will we keep track of our income and spending?
76. Will we pool all our money or have separate accounts?
77. If so, how do we share expenses?
78. Do we need to follow a budget?
79. What type of budget should we use?
80. Will we work together to create a budget?
81. How will we keep track of our budget throughout the month?
82. Is giving a part of our budget?
83. How often will we discuss the budget?
84. What would you change about our budget?
85. What keeps you up at night about our finances?
86. Is there anything about my spending you want to talk about?
87. What's one money habit that you admire about me?
88. What is the maximum amount one of us can spend without

consulting the other?
89. What's the minimum amount of money we need each month to keep your financial life afloat?
90. Should we have equal say in our finances, even if one person makes more money than the other?
91. What will we do if we disagree about our family's finances or a big purchase?
92. What would we do if one of us lost our job or both of us?
93. What do you like about the way we have been managing our money so far?
94. Is there anything you would change about how we handle money as a couple?
95. How do you feel about renting or owning a home?
96. What do you want our money to do for us that it hasn't done yet?
97. How are we planning for retirement?
98. When do we want to retire? How do we need to plan to make that a reality?
99. Are we saving for retirement?
100. What percentage of our income should we dedicate to retirement?
101. What kind of lifestyle do we want to live in retirement, and will we be able to afford it with our current savings plan?
102. Should we manage our retirement accounts on our own or hire someone to do it?
103. What are our long-term savings goals?
104. Do we plan on leaving any money behind when we die?
105. Is there a will or a beneficiary we need to set up to make that happen?
106. Do you expect to get an inheritance from your family?
107. Are there any things to consider financially as our parents

get older?
108. What does wealth mean to you?
109. Are you currently investing?
110. Is investing important to you?
111. Are you conservative or aggressive when choosing investments?
112. Will we both be responsible for investing in our future?
113. Should we manage investment accounts on our own or hire someone to do it?
114. What percentage of our income should we dedicate to investments?
115. What are the top financial concerns you have about investing?
116. Would we seek financial counseling if you needed it?
117. What type of investments do you want to use moving forward?
118. What financial goals are a priority for you?
119. How often will we talk about our finances and money goals?
120. When will we talk about money next?

The 30 Questions To Ask Yourself Before Everything & Anything

As Alex gazed out of the window, rain lightly tapping against the glass, memories floated to the forefront of his mind. When he first met Jamie, everything was new, exhilarating, and full of promise. But as the months turned to years, and talks of moving in together began to surface, a knot formed in his stomach. "Am I truly ready?" he whispered to himself, grappling with a mixture of excitement, fear, and self-reflection.

Sometimes, in the whirlwind romance of a relationship, we're swept away by the idea of "the next step." Yet, not every move is just about logistical readiness or being madly in love. It's about personal preparedness, understanding our motivations, and ensuring our own emotional and mental well-being.

You might recall Alex's dilemma. It's a common one, faced by many who stand on the precipice of major relationship milestones. This chapter is not about doubting love or the strength of a relationship. Instead, it's a gentle prompt for introspection, ensuring that when you take that step, it's with both feet firmly grounded.

Such introspection can lead to growth, clarity, and a deeper understanding of oneself and one's partner. Moving in together is a dance of two souls, and for it to be harmonious, both partners need to be in tune - not just with each other but also with themselves.

Here are 30 Questions to guide you through this soul-searching journey:

1. Why do I want to move in with my partner?
2. Am I doing this out of love or out of convenience?
3. Do I feel any external pressure to take this step?
4. How do I handle change, and am I ready for this one?
5. Am I running to something or away from something?
6. What are my major concerns about living together?
7. Am I ready to share my space daily with another person?
8. How do I feel about my partner's habits and quirks?
9. What am I hoping will change after moving in, and is that realistic?
10. How do I handle conflicts, and can I handle them constructively with my partner?
11. Am I financially stable, and am I comfortable discussing finances with my partner?
12. What are my boundaries, and have I communicated them clearly?
13. How do I envision our daily life together?
14. What are my personal and relationship goals, and are they aligned?
15. Do I have any unresolved issues or baggage that I need to address first?
16. How do I plan to maintain my personal space and independence?
17. How do I feel about our respective families' involvement

in our lives?
18. What sacrifices am I making, and am I okay with them?
19. Am I ready to accept and navigate through our differences daily?
20. How have we handled challenges in the past, and what did I learn from them?
21. Do I trust my partner completely?
22. How do we both handle stress, and can we support each other during tough times?
23. What are the non-negotiables in our relationship and living situation?
24. How do I feel about splitting household responsibilities?
25. Am I holding onto any resentments that I need to let go of or address?
26. How do I feel about our intimacy and connection levels right now?
27. Am I open to seeking relationship counseling or guidance if needed?
28. What's my gut feeling about this decision?
29. How do I feel about the future and growing old with my partner?
30. Finally, can I communicate openly with my partner about all these questions and concerns?

Like Alex, taking a moment to introspect can be invaluable. Reflect on these questions, not in doubt, but in assurance. Assure yourself that when you take this step, it's one toward mutual growth, understanding, and an ever-deepening bond. Remember, it's okay to take your time, it's okay to be sure. Your heart, mind, and soul will thank you for it.

Made in the USA
Coppell, TX
05 March 2024